nickelodeon

nick 90s
MAD LIBS

by Gabriella DeGennaro

MAD LIBS
An Imprint of Penguin Random House LLC, New York

Mad Libs format copyright © 2020 by Penguin Random House LLC. All rights reserved.

Concept created by Roger Price & Leonard Stern

Published by Mad Libs,
an imprint of Penguin Random House LLC, New York.
Printed in the USA.

Visit us online at www.penguinrandomhouse.com.

ISBN 9780593096284
1 3 5 7 9 10 8 6 4 2

MAD●LIBS®
INSTRUCTIONS

MAD LIBS® is a game for people who don't like games! It can be played by one, two, three, four, or forty.

• RIDICULOUSLY SIMPLE DIRECTIONS

In this tablet you will find stories containing blank spaces where words are left out. One player, the READER, selects one of these stories. The READER does not tell anyone what the story is about. Instead, he/she asks the other players, the WRITERS, to give him/her words. These words are used to fill in the blank spaces in the story.

• TO PLAY

The READER asks each WRITER in turn to call out a word—an adjective or a noun or whatever the space calls for—and uses them to fill in the blank spaces in the story. The result is a MAD LIBS® game.

When the READER then reads the completed MAD LIBS® game to the other players, they will discover that they have written a story that is fantastic, screamingly funny, shocking, silly, crazy, or just plain dumb—depending upon which words each WRITER called out.

• EXAMPLE (*Before* and *After*)

"_____!" he said _____
     EXCLAMATION   ADVERB

as he jumped into his convertible _____ and
                                    NOUN

drove off with his _____ wife.
                    ADJECTIVE

"____OUCH____!" he said ____HAPPILY____
     EXCLAMATION   ADVERB

as he jumped into his convertible ____CAT____ and
                                    NOUN

drove off with his ____BRAVE____ wife.
                    ADJECTIVE

MAD☉LIBS®

QUICK REVIEW

In case you have forgotten what adjectives, adverbs, nouns, and verbs are, here is a quick review:

An ADJECTIVE describes something or somebody. *Lumpy, soft, ugly, messy,* and *short* are adjectives.

An ADVERB tells how something is done. It modifies a verb and usually ends in "ly." *Modestly, stupidly, greedily,* and *carefully* are adverbs.

A NOUN is the name of a person, place, or thing. *Sidewalk, umbrella, bridle, bathtub,* and *nose* are nouns.

A VERB is an action word. *Run, pitch, jump,* and *swim* are verbs. Put the verbs in past tense if the directions say PAST TENSE. *Ran, pitched, jumped,* and *swam* are verbs in the past tense.

When we ask for A PLACE, we mean any sort of place: a country or city (*Spain, Cleveland*) or a room (*bathroom, kitchen*).

An EXCLAMATION or SILLY WORD is any sort of funny sound, gasp, grunt, or outcry, like *Wow!, Ouch!, Whomp!, Ick!,* and *Gadzooks!*

When we ask for specific words, like a NUMBER, a COLOR, an ANIMAL, or a PART OF THE BODY, we mean a word that is one of those things, like *seven, blue, horse,* or *head.*

When we ask for a PLURAL, it means more than one. For example, *cat* pluralized is *cats.*

MAD LIBS® is fun to play with friends, but you can also play it by yourself! To begin with, DO NOT look at the story on the page below. Fill in the blanks on this page with the words called for. Then, using the words you have selected, fill in the blank spaces in the story.

Now you've created your own hilarious MAD LIBS® game!

NICK-NICK-NICKELODEON

NUMBER _____

NOUN _____

VERB _____

ADJECTIVE _____

FIRST NAME _____

EXCLAMATION _____

ADJECTIVE _____

TYPE OF CONTAINER _____

LETTER OF THE ALPHABET _____

PERSON IN ROOM _____

VERB _____

ARTICLE OF CLOTHING (PLURAL) _____

SILLY WORD _____

ADJECTIVE _____

VERB _____

PART OF THE BODY _____

VEHICLE _____

ANIMAL (PLURAL) _____

Only _____ minutes left till the school _____ rings,
NUMBER   NOUN

and when it does, I'm *so* out of here! It's impossible to _____ on
VERB

algebra when I could be home watching shows like *The* _____
ADJECTIVE

Thornberrys on _____-toons. Seriously, right now the
FIRST NAME

only thing standing between me, _____ *Arnold!,*
EXCLAMATION

and an ice-_____ juice _____ is math!
ADJECTIVE   TYPE OF CONTAINER

O-M-_____! What if my older sister _____
LETTER OF THE ALPHABET   PERSON IN ROOM

makes it home before I do? She'll totally _____ the remote,
VERB

and I'd rather eat my own _____ than miss an
ARTICLE OF CLOTHING (PLURAL)

episode of *Ren &* _____ or *The* _____ *Beavers.*
SILLY WORD   ADJECTIVE

And does she actually think she can just _____ my
VERB

Fruit by the _____ and keep me from watching
PART OF THE BODY

_____ *Power?* As if! She may be bossy like Angelica
VEHICLE

from the *Rug-*_____, but I've got Mom's number on
ANIMAL (PLURAL)

speed dial!

From NICKELODEON NICK 90S MAD LIBS® • © 2020 Viacom International Inc.
Published by Mad Libs, an imprint of Penguin Random House LLC.

MAD LIBS® is fun to play with friends, but you can also play it by yourself! To begin with, DO NOT look at the story on the page below. Fill in the blanks on this page with the words called for. Then, using the words you have selected, fill in the blank spaces in the story.

Now you've created your own hilarious MAD LIBS® game!

LET'S TALK RUGRATS

VERB _____

PERSON IN ROOM _____

ANIMAL _____

VERB _____

SAME ANIMAL (PLURAL) _____

PART OF THE BODY (PLURAL) _____

ADVERB _____

VERB _____

NOUN _____

VERB (PAST TENSE) _____

NOUN _____

PART OF THE BODY _____

PLURAL NOUN _____

NOUN _____

NOUN _____

MAD LIBS

LET'S TALK RUGRATS

Tommy: _____ up, babies. We gots to get some of

VERB

_____ 's _____ food.

PERSON IN ROOM   ANIMAL

Chuckie: Why would you wanna _____ that stuff?

VERB

Tommy: If we eat his food, we'll turn into _____ just

SAME ANIMAL (PLURAL)

like him!

Phil: You mean we could scratch our _____ like we

PART OF THE BODY (PLURAL)

have fleas?

Lil: And bark as _____ as we want?

ADVERB

Tommy: Yep! But first, we gotta bust outta this playpen and

_____ into the kitchen.

VERB

Chuckie: But, Tommy, the food's way up on that _____ .

NOUN

Tommy: Chuckie! Don't you wanna lick people without getting

_____ at and wear a/an _____ around your

VERB (PAST TENSE)   NOUN

_____ with your name on it?

PART OF THE BODY

Lil: Yeah, but we're just _____ . We'll never reach that food.

PLURAL NOUN

Tommy: We may be babies, but this baby's gotta do what a/an

_____ 's gotta do! Now let's go get that dog _____ !

NOUN   NOUN

From NICKELODEON NICK 90S MAD LIBS® • © 2020 Viacom International Inc.
Published by Mad Libs, an imprint of Penguin Random House LLC.

MAD LIBS® is fun to play with friends, but you can also play it by yourself! To begin with, DO NOT look at the story on the page below. Fill in the blanks on this page with the words called for. Then, using the words you have selected, fill in the blank spaces in the story.

Now you've created your own hilarious MAD LIBS® game!

ARNOLD, MY LOVE

PERSON IN ROOM _____

PART OF THE BODY _____

VERB _____

ADJECTIVE _____

TYPE OF FOOD _____

PART OF THE BODY _____

SAME PERSON IN ROOM _____

PLURAL NOUN _____

COLOR _____

ADJECTIVE _____

PART OF THE BODY (PLURAL) _____

NOUN _____

PLURAL NOUN _____

ADJECTIVE _____

PLURAL NOUN _____

PLURAL NOUN _____

ADVERB _____

CELEBRITY _____

MAD LIBS®

ARNOLD, MY LOVE

Oh, _____ . My _____ aches as I write your
　　　PERSON IN ROOM　　　　　PART OF THE BODY

name in the pages of this diary. A name I dare not _____ .
　　　　　　　　　　　　　　　　　　　　　　　　　　　VERB

Oh how I long for the day when you'll rescue me from this

_____ life of beepers and blues. And yet, I'm urged to
ADJECTIVE

deliver but one knuckle _____ to your precious football-
　　　　　　　　　　　　TYPE OF FOOD

shaped _____ . _____ , you idiot. Just
　　　PART OF THE BODY　　　SAME PERSON IN ROOM

thinking of your cornflower _____ and eyes like
　　　　　　　　　　　　　　　　PLURAL NOUN

sprawling fields of _____ , I grow _____ . Or
　　　　　　　　　COLOR　　　　　　　　ADJECTIVE

perhaps your _____ are more like pools of
　　　　　　PART OF THE BODY (PLURAL)

_____ ? I could swim for days, months, _____
NOUN　　　　　　　　　　　　　　　　　　　　　PLURAL NOUN

and never tire. When will you notice me, my darling? Your red,

_____ lips look like _____ . I could spend an
ADJECTIVE　　　　　　　　PLURAL NOUN

eternity counting the _____ till you are mine, but until
　　　　　　　　　　PLURAL NOUN

then I'm afraid you make me _____ wacky. Someday I'll
　　　　　　　　　　　　　　ADVERB

tell the whole world of our love or my name isn't _____
　　　　　　　　　　　　　　　　　　　　　　　　CELEBRITY

G. Pataki!

From NICKELODEON NICK 90S MAD LIBS® • © 2020 Viacom International Inc.
Published by Mad Libs, an imprint of Penguin Random House LLC.

MAD LIBS® is fun to play with friends, but you can also play it by yourself! To begin with, DO NOT look at the story on the page below. Fill in the blanks on this page with the words called for. Then, using the words you have selected, fill in the blank spaces in the story.

Now you've created your own hilarious MAD LIBS® game!

BEAVER BROTHER MIX-UP

PLURAL NOUN _____

ADJECTIVE _____

ANIMAL _____

NUMBER _____

ADJECTIVE _____

ADJECTIVE _____

TYPE OF FOOD (PLURAL) _____

NOUN _____

ADVERB _____

VERB _____

VERB _____

ADJECTIVE _____

ADJECTIVE _____

COLOR _____

PLURAL NOUN _____

ANIMAL _____

MAD LIBS®

BEAVER BROTHER MIX-UP

Norbert and Daggett may be _____ , but these
                                    PLURAL NOUN
_____ beavers are anything but identical. Can you tell
      ADJECTIVE
them apart?

1. Which _____ , born _____ minutes earlier, is the
              ANIMAL   NUMBER
   _____ , older brother? (a) Norbert, (b) Daggett
        ADJECTIVE

2. The _____ catchphrase "That was _____ !"
          ADJECTIVE   TYPE OF FOOD (PLURAL)
   belongs to . . . (a) Daggett, (b) Norbert

3. Which _____ is more likely to pull you in and say
                NOUN
   _____ , "Biiiiig hug!"? (a) Norbert, (b) Daggett
        ADVERB

4. Do *not* _____ this brother's hair, or else he will
                  VERB
   _____ . (a) Norbert, (b) Daggett
        VERB

5. A red _____ nose, _____ , pointy teeth, and
              ADJECTIVE   ADJECTIVE
   _____ hair belong to . . . (a) Daggett, (b) Norbert
      COLOR

If you guessed *a* for each of the _____ , welcome to
                                        PLURAL NOUN
the _____ family!
        ANIMAL

From NICKELODEON NICK 90S MAD LIBS® • © 2020 Viacom International Inc.
Published by Mad Libs, an imprint of Penguin Random House LLC.

MAD LIBS® is fun to play with friends, but you can also play it by yourself! To begin with, DO NOT look at the story on the page below. Fill in the blanks on this page with the words called for. Then, using the words you have selected, fill in the blank spaces in the story.

Now you've created your own hilarious MAD LIBS® game!

CLASS WITH THE GROMBLE

PLURAL NOUN _____

ADJECTIVE _____

COLOR _____

PLURAL NOUN _____

VERB _____

PART OF THE BODY _____

CELEBRITY _____

VERB ENDING IN "ING" _____

NUMBER _____

VERB ENDING IN "ING" _____

PLURAL NOUN _____

ADJECTIVE _____

ARTICLE OF CLOTHING (PLURAL) _____

NUMBER _____

VERB ENDING IN "ING" _____

PLURAL NOUN _____

ADJECTIVE _____

MAD LIBS®

CLASS WITH THE GROMBLE

Settle down, _____. It's time for class. _____
                PLURAL NOUN   ADJECTIVE

morning, isn't it? Dark, _____, and hideous, just the way
                          COLOR

I like it. As a reminder, there's no passing _____ in
                                              PLURAL NOUN

class. The last amusing little note I found read "The Gromble likes to

_____." A lovely sentiment because I DO and I WILL!
    VERB

Now, if you'd like to keep your _____ attached to your
                                 PART OF THE BODY

neck, unlike poor _____, I suggest _____
                   CELEBRITY   VERB ENDING IN "ING"

your monster manual to page _____ so we can begin
                             NUMBER

class. _____ humans comes naturally for us
        VERB ENDING IN "ING"

_____, but it's a craft you must perfect! How can you
 PLURAL NOUN

expect to give anyone the _____ crawlies if you can't even
                           ADJECTIVE

scare the _____ off a/an _____ -year-
           ARTICLE OF CLOTHING (PLURAL)   NUMBER

old? Did you think _____ was going to be easy?
                    VERB ENDING IN "ING"

WRONG! First rule, and write this down: Never question my

_____, because the Gromble is ALWAYS RIGHT! Class
 PLURAL NOUN

dismissed, you _____ worms!
                ADJECTIVE

From NICKELODEON NICK 90S MAD LIBS® • © 2020 Viacom International Inc.
Published by Mad Libs, an imprint of Penguin Random House LLC.

MAD LIBS® is fun to play with friends, but you can also play it by yourself! To begin with, DO NOT look at the story on the page below. Fill in the blanks on this page with the words called for. Then, using the words you have selected, fill in the blank spaces in the story.

Now you've created your own hilarious MAD LIBS® game!

ROCKO'S LAUNDRY LESSONS

A PLACE _____

ADJECTIVE _____

ADJECTIVE _____

COLOR _____

PLURAL NOUN _____

ANIMAL _____

NOUN _____

NOUN _____

ADJECTIVE _____

VERB ENDING IN "ING" _____

VERB _____

VERB _____

CELEBRITY _____

PLURAL NOUN _____

VERB _____

ARTICLE OF CLOTHING (PLURAL) _____

NOUN _____

MAD LIBS

ROCKO'S LAUNDRY LESSONS

Rocko here! These are a few tips for surviving modern life in (the)

_____ , because after all, laundry day is a very _____

A PLACE   ADJECTIVE

day.

Do take your _____ clothes to the laundromat once they've

ADJECTIVE

started dripping _____ sludge.

COLOR

Don't wait till your _____ pile up and capture your

PLURAL NOUN

_____ . (Sorry, Spunky!)

ANIMAL

Do wear a/an _____ mask while using a/an _____

NOUN   NOUN

to shovel your filthy clothes into _____-duty bags.

ADJECTIVE

Don't lose control of your _____ machine! Beware:

VERB ENDING IN "ING"

It could _____ your laundry buddy and _____

VERB   VERB

down the street!

Do bring a buddy to help you. I've got my dog, _____ .

CELEBRITY

And finally, **don't** let the Gripes steal your _____ ! Those

PLURAL NOUN

creatures hide in the washer just waiting to _____ your

VERB

socks and ruin your _____ !

ARTICLE OF CLOTHING (PLURAL)

Remember: If you can survive _____ day, you can do anything!

NOUN

MAD LIBS® is fun to play with friends, but you can also play it by yourself! To begin with, DO NOT look at the story on the page below. Fill in the blanks on this page with the words called for. Then, using the words you have selected, fill in the blank spaces in the story.

Now you've created your own hilarious MAD LIBS® game!

HIDE-AND-REPTAR, BY TOMMY

VERB _____

COLOR _____

FIRST NAME _____

TYPE OF FOOD _____

PERSON IN ROOM _____

VERB _____

A PLACE _____

NOUN _____

ADJECTIVE _____

NOUN _____

NOUN _____

SILLY WORD _____

CELEBRITY _____

ANIMAL _____

ARTICLE OF CLOTHING _____

EXCLAMATION _____

ADJECTIVE _____

VERB _____

MAD LIBS®
HIDE-AND-REPTAR, BY TOMMY

It all started with a game of _____ -and-seek to find Reptar.
                                    VERB

He's the big, _____ T. _____ that's on TV and
                COLOR   FIRST NAME

_____ boxes. My cousin _____ said some mean
TYPE OF FOOD   PERSON IN ROOM

stuff about him that made me _____. I was sad, but
                               VERB

Chuckie cheered me up. He thought Reptar might be hiding in

(the) _____. We searched everywhere, even behind the
       A PLACE

_____, but we couldn't find him. I was ready to give up,
NOUN

but then I saw it. A/An _____ baby Reptar climbing up a/an
                         ADJECTIVE

_____. It was smaller than a/an _____, but looked
NOUN   NOUN

just like the real _____. Phil and _____ wanted to
                    SILLY WORD   CELEBRITY

hold it, but Chuckie heard my mommy coming. I had to think

fast! I put the _____ in my _____ and
                 ANIMAL   ARTICLE OF CLOTHING

_____! It felt _____ hiding it in my diaper, but
EXCLAMATION   ADJECTIVE

it worked! Back inside, we were so worried about Reptar, but we did

what us babies had to do: _____ that dinosaur and bring
                           VERB

that baby back!

From NICKELODEON NICK 90S MAD LIBS® • © 2020 Viacom International Inc.
Published by Mad Libs, an imprint of Penguin Random House LLC.

MAD LIBS® is fun to play with friends, but you can also play it by yourself! To begin with, DO NOT look at the story on the page below. Fill in the blanks on this page with the words called for. Then, using the words you have selected, fill in the blank spaces in the story.

Now you've created your own hilarious MAD LIBS® game!

THIS IS ME, ELIZA THORNBERRY

PERSON IN ROOM _____

TYPE OF FOOD _____

OCCUPATION _____

NOUN _____

ANIMAL (PLURAL) _____

VERB (PAST TENSE) _____

NOUN _____

CELEBRITY _____

ANIMAL _____

TYPE OF BUILDING _____

VERB _____

NOUN _____

VERB ENDING IN "S" _____

ADJECTIVE _____

NOUN _____

VERB _____

ADJECTIVE _____

EXCLAMATION _____

MAD LIBS
THIS IS ME,
ELIZA THORNBERRY

This is me, _____ Thorn-_____. I come
            PERSON IN ROOM   TYPE OF FOOD

from a pretty average family. I've got a dad, a/an _____,
                                                    OCCUPATION

a sister, and a little _____ named Donnie. He was being
                           NOUN

raised by _____ when we _____ him. I
          ANIMAL (PLURAL)   VERB (PAST TENSE)

also have a best _____ named _____, who happens
                    NOUN   CELEBRITY

to be a/an _____. We live in a/an _____
              ANIMAL   TYPE OF BUILDING

on wheels and _____ around the world because my dad
                  VERB

hosts a/an _____ show and my mom _____
              NOUN   VERB ENDING IN "S"

it. Okay, so maybe we're not *that* average. And—between you and

me—something _____ happened when I met a/an
                  ADJECTIVE

_____ in Africa. Now I can _____ to animals;
    NOUN   VERB

it's really _____, but totally secret! _____!
              ADJECTIVE   EXCLAMATION

MAD LIBS® is fun to play with friends, but you can also play it by yourself! To begin with, DO NOT look at the story on the page below. Fill in the blanks on this page with the words called for. Then, using the words you have selected, fill in the blank spaces in the story.

Now you've created your own hilarious MAD LIBS® game!

REN OR STIMPY?

NOUN _____

ADJECTIVE _____

NOUN _____

ADVERB _____

NOUN _____

TYPE OF FOOD _____

VERB _____

ADVERB _____

EXCLAMATION _____

NOUN _____

VERB _____

NOUN _____

VERB _____

ADJECTIVE _____

PLURAL NOUN _____

ADJECTIVE _____

NOUN _____

MAD LIBS

REN OR STIMPY?

Answer these questions with your closest _____ to find out
                                              NOUN
if you're more like Ren or Stimpy.

1. You're . . . (a) A dog person! Cats are _____!
                                              ADJECTIVE

   (b) A cat _____! Chihuahuas are _____ yappy!
              NOUN   ADVERB

2. If your best _____ accidentally eats the _____
                  NOUN   TYPE OF FOOD
   you've been saving, you (a) Call them an eediot! How dare they

   _____ your food! (b) Shrug _____ and say,
         VERB   ADVERB

   "_____, I don't care!"
        EXCLAMATION

3. When your _____ disagrees with you, you . . .
                  NOUN

   (a) _____! They must be a/an _____ who doesn't
          VERB   NOUN

   know who they're dealing with! (b) _____ your favorite
                                          VERB

   song, "Happy _____ Joy Joy"!
                  ADJECTIVE

If you answered *a* for most of the _____, you're just like
                                       PLURAL NOUN

Ren—ill-tempered, hyper, and _____. If you chose mostly
                               ADJECTIVE

b's, you may not be the sharpest _____ in the shed but,
                                      NOUN

like Stimpy, you're a good friend!

MAD LIBS® is fun to play with friends, but you can also play it by yourself! To begin with, DO NOT look at the story on the page below. Fill in the blanks on this page with the words called for. Then, using the words you have selected, fill in the blank spaces in the story.

Now you've created your own hilarious MAD LIBS® game!

BEEFING IT WITH
ROCKET POWER!

NOUN _____

OCCUPATION _____

ADVERB _____

NOUN _____

NUMBER _____

VERB ENDING IN "ING" _____

ANIMAL _____

VERB ENDING IN "ING" _____

NOUN _____

VERB _____

PLURAL NOUN _____

TYPE OF BUILDING _____

VERB _____

ADJECTIVE _____

NUMBER _____

PLURAL NOUN _____

NOUN _____

VERB _____

MAD LIBS
BEEFING IT WITH
ROCKET POWER!

Otto _____ may be Ocean Shores' sickest surfer,
         NOUN

_____, and skater, but that doesn't mean he's never
OCCUPATION

_____ beefed it. Usually Rocket Boy can brush it off and keep
ADVERB

shredding, but how can he when his best _____ Twister's got
                                          NOUN

_____ gnarly minutes of Otto _____ -out recorded
NUMBER   VERB ENDING IN "ING"

on camera? It's typical for a dude like _____ to beef
                                          ANIMAL

it on the reg, but Otto's not trying to have his pro- _____
                                                      VERB ENDING IN "ING"

career wrecked by a video that crowns him _____ of
                                            NOUN

Shoobies! He's got to _____ that tape before Twister
                        VERB

premieres the footage to all their _____ at the Shore
                                     PLURAL NOUN

_____ ! But, if he does, he'll _____ all of
TYPE OF BUILDING   VERB

Twister's _____ work on the film, and that would be pretty
           ADJECTIVE

weak of him. Looks like there's only _____ things he can do:
                                       NUMBER

Remind those _____ that even though he may look like a
               PLURAL NOUN

total _____ whomping out on the waves, he's still totally
        NOUN

Otto-matic and will challenge anyone to a/an _____ -off to
                                               VERB

prove it!

MAD LIBS® is fun to play with friends, but you can also play it by yourself! To begin with, DO NOT look at the story on the page below. Fill in the blanks on this page with the words called for. Then, using the words you have selected, fill in the blank spaces in the story.

Now you've created your own hilarious MAD LIBS® game!

THOSE DUMB BABIES!

TYPE OF FOOD (PLURAL) _____

NOUN _____

ADJECTIVE _____

NOUN _____

ADJECTIVE _____

A PLACE _____

PERSON IN ROOM _____

PLURAL NOUN _____

VERB _____

VERB _____

ADJECTIVE _____

PART OF THE BODY (PLURAL) _____

VERB ENDING IN "ING" _____

LETTER OF THE ALPHABET _____

PLURAL NOUN _____

CELEBRITY _____

ADJECTIVE _____

ADJECTIVE _____

MAD LIBS®

THOSE DUMB BABIES!

My name's Angelica _____ but you can call me
TYPE OF FOOD (PLURAL)

angel _____ , pretty _____ princess, or
NOUN   ADJECTIVE

cupcake, because I'm the sweetest _____ you'll ever meet!
NOUN

I used to be the cutest, most _____ kid in all of (the)
ADJECTIVE

_____ , until my cousin _____ and those other
A PLACE   PERSON IN ROOM

dumb _____ came around. What do those babies do that I
PLURAL NOUN

can't? I _____ the prettiest, look the cutest, and _____
VERB   VERB

the bestest! What is there *not* to love? While those _____
ADJECTIVE

babies are sucking on their _____ and
PART OF THE BODY (PLURAL)

_____ in their diapers, I'm on my way to becoming
VERB ENDING IN "ING"

the next CE-_____ of Super _____
LETTER OF THE ALPHABET   PLURAL NOUN

and Glitter—just like my mommy! So what if I'm a little bossy? Me

and my doll, _____ , are gonna be _____ one
CELEBRITY   ADJECTIVE

day, so you better forget those _____ crybabies and
ADJECTIVE

remember me: Angelica!

From NICKELODEON NICK 90S MAD LIBS® • © 2020 Viacom International Inc.
Published by Mad Libs, an imprint of Penguin Random House LLC.

MAD LIBS® is fun to play with friends, but you can also play it by yourself! To begin with, DO NOT look at the story on the page below. Fill in the blanks on this page with the words called for. Then, using the words you have selected, fill in the blank spaces in the story.

Now you've created your own hilarious MAD LIBS® game!

NICK 90S PETS

NOUN _____

ADJECTIVE _____

NOUN _____

ADJECTIVE _____

NOUN _____

ADJECTIVE _____

VERB _____

ADJECTIVE _____

NOUN _____

CITY _____

ANIMAL (PLURAL) _____

VERB _____

TYPE OF FOOD (PLURAL) _____

ADJECTIVE _____

ADVERB _____

MAD LIBS®
NICK 90S PETS

Read the mystery clues below to guess the 1990s Nick pet:

1. This adorable potbellied _____ is sweet, _____,
   <u>NOUN</u>   <u>ADJECTIVE</u>

   and brings the country to Hill-_____ .
                                    <u>NOUN</u>

2. Looking for _____ conversation? We've got a talkative
                <u>ADJECTIVE</u>

   _____ for you who loves to monkey around.
    <u>NOUN</u>

3. Loyal, _____ , and great with babies who like to
           <u>ADJECTIVE</u>

   _____ around?! Sounds perfect!
    <u>VERB</u>

4. So _____ , he could fit into your _____ !
      <u>ADJECTIVE</u>   <u>NOUN</u>

Answer Key:

1. Most apartments in _____ don't allow cats or
                       <u>CITY</u>

   _____ in the building, but they didn't say anything
   <u>ANIMAL (PLURAL)</u>

   about pigs! "Oink" if you love Abner!

2. Get ready to _____ , because Darwin is one chatty
                 <u>VERB</u>

   chimpanzee.

3. Part of the _____ family, Spike is a very
                <u>TYPE OF FOOD (PLURAL)</u>

   _____ dog!
   <u>ADJECTIVE</u>

4. Spunky's name fits his personality _____ !
                                       <u>ADVERB</u>

From NICKELODEON NICK 90S MAD LIBS® • © 2020 Viacom International Inc.
Published by Mad Libs, an imprint of Penguin Random House LLC.

MAD LIBS® is fun to play with friends, but you can also play it by yourself! To begin with, DO NOT look at the story on the page below. Fill in the blanks on this page with the words called for. Then, using the words you have selected, fill in the blank spaces in the story.

Now you've created your own hilarious MAD LIBS® game!

BEAVER BROTHER BLUES

NOUN _____

ADJECTIVE _____

ANIMAL _____

VERB (PAST TENSE) _____

LETTER OF THE ALPHABET _____

ADJECTIVE _____

VERB ENDING IN "ING" _____

TYPE OF FOOD _____

NOUN _____

ADJECTIVE _____

NOUN _____

ADJECTIVE _____

VERB _____

ADJECTIVE _____

ADJECTIVE _____

ADJECTIVE _____

MAD LIBS®

BEAVER BROTHER BLUES

Oh, hello there. Norbert _____ here. I know what you're
                          NOUN

thinking: It must be pretty cool being a/an _____ bra-ther
                                            ADJECTIVE

to a young, impressionable _____. Sure it's got its perks,
                           ANIMAL

but it's not all it's _____ up to be. For one thing, little
                      VERB (PAST TENSE)

Daggy- _____ can be quite the prankster. It's
       LETTER OF THE ALPHABET

hard to keep things chill and stay _____ when Dag is
                                   ADJECTIVE

_____ around cramping my style. I mean, I try my
VERB ENDING IN "ING"

best to be as cool as a/an _____, but it must be hard having
                          TYPE OF FOOD

an older _____ as smart and as _____-looking as
         NOUN   ADJECTIVE

me. Poor little guy, no matter how hard he tries, his _____
                                                      NOUN

will never be as _____ as my luscious blond locks. But
                 ADJECTIVE

every once in a while I _____ myself and feel the
                        VERB

_____ love between my _____ roommate and
ADJECTIVE   ADJECTIVE

me. I know Daggy-aggy loves his _____ hugs.
                                ADJECTIVE

MAD LIBS® is fun to play with friends, but you can also play it by yourself! To begin with, DO NOT look at the story on the page below. Fill in the blanks on this page with the words called for. Then, using the words you have selected, fill in the blank spaces in the story.

Now you've created your own hilarious MAD LIBS® game!

DINNER WITH ARNOLD

TYPE OF BUILDING _____

NUMBER _____

NOUN _____

ADJECTIVE _____

VERB ENDING IN "ING" _____

PERSON IN ROOM _____

ANIMAL _____

ADJECTIVE _____

NOUN _____

PLURAL NOUN _____

EXCLAMATION _____

VERB ENDING IN "ING" _____

ADJECTIVE _____

NOUN _____

ADJECTIVE _____

COLOR _____

TYPE OF FOOD (PLURAL) _____

ADJECTIVE _____

MAD LIBS®

DINNER WITH ARNOLD

Sure, some people have quiet family dinners, but at the boarding-

_____ we do things a little differently. For starters,
TYPE OF BUILDING

there's _____ of us gathered around the _____ every
NUMBER   NOUN

night. It may be a/an _____ table, but the personalities in
ADJECTIVE

the room are even bigger. Between Mr. Hyunh _____
VERB ENDING IN "ING"

about his day at El Patio, _____ begging Suzie for more
PERSON IN ROOM

money, and Ernie chewing like a/an _____, I'd say things
ANIMAL

can get pretty _____. Oh, and there's also my grandpa
ADJECTIVE

and _____. Grandpa loves to tell long stories about
NOUN

_____. _____! For a man who is
PLURAL NOUN   EXCLAMATION

_____ his teeth, he sure can talk! And Grandma—
VERB ENDING IN "ING"

well, let's just say she's the most _____ _____ I know.
ADJECTIVE   NOUN

She may look _____, but she's got a/an _____
ADJECTIVE   COLOR

belt in martial arts and packs a bigger punch than her spicy

_____. We might not all be related, but we act like
TYPE OF FOOD (PLURAL)

one _____ family.
ADJECTIVE

From NICKELODEON NICK 90S MAD LIBS® • © 2020 Viacom International Inc.
Published by Mad Libs, an imprint of Penguin Random House LLC.

MAD LIBS® is fun to play with friends, but you can also play it by yourself! To begin with, DO NOT look at the story on the page below. Fill in the blanks on this page with the words called for. Then, using the words you have selected, fill in the blank spaces in the story.

Now you've created your own hilarious MAD LIBS® game!

GRITTY KITTY LITTER, BY STIMPSON J. CAT

VERB _____

ANIMAL _____

OCCUPATION _____

VERB _____

VERB ENDING IN "ING" _____

ADJECTIVE _____

ANIMAL _____

VERB _____

PART OF THE BODY _____

VERB _____

ADJECTIVE _____

ADJECTIVE _____

NOUN _____

ADJECTIVE _____

PLURAL NOUN _____

ADJECTIVE _____

OCCUPATION _____

ADJECTIVE _____

MAD LIBS
GRITTY KITTY LITTER,
BY STIMPSON J. CAT

Oh joy! I'm so glad you're going to _____ my poem about
_____ VERB
_____ litter. Ren seems a little jealous of me as a fancy
ANIMAL
_____ , but what can I say? I _____ this stuff so
OCCUPATION   VERB
much that the words are just _____ out of me!
                            VERB ENDING IN "ING"

Gritty Kitty ain't so _____ , but it's really thick.
                      ADJECTIVE

It fills my _____ box oh so snug, it always does the trick.
           ANIMAL

I like to _____ it on my _____ , and squish,
         VERB   PART OF THE BODY

and _____ , and squish.
    VERB

It ne'er offends my _____ nose, like a/an _____ fish!
                    ADJECTIVE   ADJECTIVE

Its _____ is a joy to me, it's just as _____ as silk.
    NOUN   ADJECTIVE

It makes my little _____ twitch, it stays _____ ,
                   PLURAL NOUN   ADJECTIVE

even in milk!

I may not be the _____ , I may not be the pope.
                 OCCUPATION

But as long as I have _____ Kitty, I shall never mope!
                      ADJECTIVE

MAD LIBS® is fun to play with friends, but you can also play it by yourself! To begin with, DO NOT look at the story on the page below. Fill in the blanks on this page with the words called for. Then, using the words you have selected, fill in the blank spaces in the story.

Now you've created your own hilarious MAD LIBS® game!

I'LL BE IN MY ROOM!

NOUN _____

ADJECTIVE _____

NOUN _____

NOUN _____

ADJECTIVE _____

PLURAL NOUN _____

ADJECTIVE _____

ADJECTIVE _____

NOUN _____

VERB ENDING IN "ING" _____

ANIMAL _____

NOUN _____

NOUN _____

VERB _____

PLURAL NOUN _____

ADJECTIVE _____

VERB ENDING IN "ING" _____

VEHICLE _____

MAD LIBS®

I'LL BE IN MY ROOM!

I'm Debbie _____-berry, and I am anything but a/an
                    NOUN

_____ teenage _____. Normal teenagers have their
   ADJECTIVE   NOUN

own _____-rooms, go to _____ school with cute
        NOUN   ADJECTIVE

_____, and have best friends that aren't their annoying
   PLURAL NOUN

_____ siblings. It's so unfair! Because of my dad's
   ADJECTIVE

_____ nature show, I've had to waste my prime years in a
   ADJECTIVE

camper the size of a/an _____-box. There's no privacy—
                            NOUN

I mean, you try _____ a bathroom with a/an
                VERB ENDING IN "ING"

_____ your sister calls a pet. I love my family and all, but
   ANIMAL

I need some _____ and quiet, which is *way* hard to find
                NOUN

when your whole family shares one _____. Like, how am I
                                        NOUN

supposed to _____ my magazines and keep up with
                VERB

fashion trends if everyone's always blabbing on about animals and

_____? Traveling is _____, I guess, but I'd much
   PLURAL NOUN   ADJECTIVE

rather settle into suburbia. Like, imagine me _____ to
                                              VERB ENDING IN "ING"

the mall in a/an _____ that's all mine?! A girl can only
                    VEHICLE

dream . . . in her shared bedroom. UGH!

MAD LIBS® is fun to play with friends, but you can also play it by yourself! To begin with, DO NOT look at the story on the page below. Fill in the blanks on this page with the words called for. Then, using the words you have selected, fill in the blank spaces in the story.

Now you've created your own hilarious MAD LIBS® game!

SCARE TACTICS

NOUN _____

EXCLAMATION _____

VERB ENDING IN "ING" _____

NOUN _____

NOUN _____

ADJECTIVE _____

VERB _____

NUMBER _____

PLURAL NOUN _____

NOUN _____

VERB _____

NOUN _____

PART OF THE BODY _____

PART OF THE BODY (PLURAL) _____

ADVERB _____

VERB _____

NOUN _____

MAD LIBS

SCARE TACTICS

Think you know the _____ students of _____!!!
                      NOUN   EXCLAMATION

Real Monsters well enough to tell their _____ methods
                                          VERB ENDING IN "ING"

apart? Match each _____ below with the right monster . . .
                      NOUN

if you dare!

1. This _____ may look like a/an _____
            NOUN   ADJECTIVE

   little bunny, but he'll surprise and _____ any human
                                              VERB

   when he grows _____ times in size!
                     NUMBER

2. If it's guts and _____ you fear, you might want to look
                       PLURAL NOUN

   the other way when this _____ pulls her organs out for
                               NOUN

   all to _____. And that's not all: With her ability to
             VERB

   _____ -shift, any scare is possible.
       NOUN

3. Quick, plug your _____ and shield your
                         PART OF THE BODY

   _____, because this monster is _____
     PART OF THE BODY (PLURAL)   ADVERB

   disgusting! Humans _____ in fear with just a sniff of
                           VERB

   his _____ odor.
          NOUN

Answer Key: 1. Ickis, 2. Oblina, 3. Krumm

From NICKELODEON NICK 90S MAD LIBS® • © 2020 Viacom International Inc.
Published by Mad Libs, an imprint of Penguin Random House LLC.

MAD LIBS® is fun to play with friends, but you can also play it by yourself! To begin with, DO NOT look at the story on the page below. Fill in the blanks on this page with the words called for. Then, using the words you have selected, fill in the blank spaces in the story.

Now you've created your own hilarious MAD LIBS® game!

POWER GIRL SURFERS
SHRED, BY REGGIE ROCKET

PLURAL NOUN _____

NOUN _____

VERB ENDING IN "ING" _____

NOUN _____

VERB _____

OCCUPATION (PLURAL) _____

PERSON IN ROOM _____

CITY _____

PART OF THE BODY _____

CELEBRITY _____

VERB (PAST TENSE) _____

NOUN _____

SAME PERSON IN ROOM _____

ADJECTIVE _____

VERB ENDING IN "ING" _____

NOUN _____

ADJECTIVE _____

NOUN _____

MAD LIBS
POWER GIRL SURFERS
SHRED, BY REGGIE ROCKET

Catching _____ and shredding hard isn't just for boys.
PLURAL NOUN

I'm Reggie _____, and I'm _____ to bring
NOUN   VERB ENDING IN "ING"

you the stories of the Power _____ Surfers—girls who totally
NOUN

_____! While some _____ only cover the
VERB   OCCUPATION (PLURAL)

same old status quo, the 'Zine takes a fresh look at bringing girl

surfers into the spotlight. Meet _____: She's one of
PERSON IN ROOM

_____'s raddest surfers! In a recent head-to-_____
CITY   PART OF THE BODY

with surfer _____ Rocket, she _____
CELEBRITY   VERB (PAST TENSE)

the competition so hard, there was barely anything left of his surf-

_____. _____ told the 'Zine in an exclusive
NOUN   SAME PERSON IN ROOM

interview that she's "just _____ to be both riding and
ADJECTIVE

_____ waves as a/an _____ Girl Surfer." So
VERB ENDING IN "ING"   NOUN

next time you hear someone being _____ to a totally rad
ADJECTIVE

female surfer, stand up and share this _____!
NOUN

MAD LIBS® is fun to play with friends, but you can also play it by yourself! To begin with, DO NOT look at the story on the page below. Fill in the blanks on this page with the words called for. Then, using the words you have selected, fill in the blank spaces in the story.

Now you've created your own hilarious MAD LIBS® game!

A SMASHING ANIMAL SIGHTING!

PERSON IN ROOM _____

ADJECTIVE _____

NOUN _____

A PLACE _____

SILLY WORD _____

NOUN _____

NOUN _____

PART OF THE BODY (PLURAL) _____

ADJECTIVE _____

ANIMAL (PLURAL) _____

VERB ENDING IN "ING" _____

PLURAL NOUN _____

NOUN _____

VERB ENDING IN "ING" _____

ADVERB _____

A PLACE _____

PART OF THE BODY _____

ADJECTIVE _____

Quick, _____! Grab the camera, dear, there's been a/an
　　　　PERSON IN ROOM

_____ discovery. I'm Nigel _____-berry reporting
　ADJECTIVE　　　　　　　　　　　　　　　NOUN

from the southern tip of (the) _____ , where I believe we've
　　　　　　　　　　　　　　　　A PLACE

stumbled upon the ancient ruins of _____ . Take a gander
　　　　　　　　　　　　　　　　SILLY WORD

at the lush surroundings despite years of _____ and
　　　　　　　　　　　　　　　　　　　NOUN

decay. And what's that? Zoom in on that _____! Oh my,
　　　　　　　　　　　　　　　　　　NOUN

I can't believe my _____. Now we must be
　　　　　　　PART OF THE BODY (PLURAL)

_____ as to not disturb this miraculous sighting. Most
　ADJECTIVE

_____ instinctively travel alone, but here we have a
ANIMAL (PLURAL)

peculiar pack. _____! See the mother there in the
　　　　　VERB ENDING IN "ING"

center? She's gathering _____ for her babies from the
　　　　　　　　　　PLURAL NOUN

_____ tree, which I must say is a true tropical delicacy! And
NOUN

what's this? She's _____ them with her snout? A/An
　　　　　VERB ENDING IN "ING"

_____ sophisticated technique! I must give it the old
　ADVERB

_____ try. A bit tricky with my pointy _____,
A PLACE　　　　　　　　　　　　　　　PART OF THE BODY

but I'd say I'm getting the hang of it. A really smashing, _____
　　　　　　　　　　　　　　　　　　　　ADJECTIVE

time!

MAD LIBS® is fun to play with friends, but you can also play it by yourself! To begin with, DO NOT look at the story on the page below. Fill in the blanks on this page with the words called for. Then, using the words you have selected, fill in the blank spaces in the story.

Now you've created your own hilarious MAD LIBS® game!

HEFFER'S A HOOT!

NOUN _____

PLURAL NOUN _____

ANIMAL _____

VERB (PAST TENSE) _____

PLURAL NOUN _____

VERB _____

NOUN _____

NOUN _____

SILLY WORD _____

PLURAL NOUN _____

NOUN _____

OCCUPATION _____

ADJECTIVE _____

VERB ENDING IN "ING" _____

PERSON IN ROOM _____

A PLACE _____

NOUN _____

NOUN _____

MAD LIBS

HEFFER'S A HOOT!

Hi there. I'm Heffer! I'm sure you know all about my best

_____, Rocko, but let me tell you a bit about me! Some
　　　NOUN

_____ might call me a/an _____, but I'm
　　PLURAL NOUN　　　　　　　　　　　　ANIMAL

actually a steer. Can't you tell? I was raised and _____ by
　　　　　　　　　　　　　　　　　　　　　　　VERB (PAST TENSE)

a pack of _____. They're a little wild, but, hey, they're
　　　　　PLURAL NOUN

family. My favorite thing to do is _____! I think I'm the
　　　　　　　　　　　　　　　　　VERB

only _____ that's been kicked out of the Night _____
　　　NOUN　　　　　　　　　　　　　　　　　　　　　NOUN

Diner . . . what a/an _____! I've done lots of odd
　　　　　　　　　SILLY WORD

_____: I've been everything from a farmer to a security
　PLURAL NOUN

_____ to a/an _____. Those jobs are sure fun, but
　NOUN　　　　　　OCCUPATION

what I like most is a/an _____ day just _____
　　　　　　　　　　　　ADJECTIVE　　　　　　VERB ENDING IN "ING"

around with my pal, _____. I think I'll go over to his
　　　　　　　　PERSON IN ROOM

_____ now and see if he wants to go _____-skating
　A PLACE　　　　　　　　　　　　　　　　　　NOUN

together. I don't know if you've heard, but I'm the _____ of
　　　　　　　　　　　　　　　　　　　　　　　　　NOUN

the roller rink!

MAD LIBS® is fun to play with friends, but you can also play it by yourself! To begin with, DO NOT look at the story on the page below. Fill in the blanks on this page with the words called for. Then, using the words you have selected, fill in the blank spaces in the story.

Now you've created your own hilarious MAD LIBS® game!

NICK TRIVIA

NOUN _____

PART OF THE BODY _____

ADJECTIVE _____

PLURAL NOUN _____

PERSON IN ROOM _____

NOUN _____

COLOR _____

PLURAL NOUN _____

NOUN _____

ADJECTIVE _____

CELEBRITY _____

NOUN _____

VERB ENDING IN "ING" _____

NUMBER _____

EXCLAMATION _____

VERB _____

TYPE OF FOOD _____

FIRST NAME _____

MAD LIBS®

NICK TRIVIA

Think you remember the 90s like they were yesterday? Jog your

_____ and test your _____ with this
NOUN   PART OF THE BODY

_____ trivia about your favorite Nick _____ .
ADJECTIVE   PLURAL NOUN

1. Rocko from _____ 's *Modern* _____ wears
                  PERSON IN ROOM   NOUN

   a/an _____ shirt with which type of pattern? (a) Stripes,
         COLOR

   (b) Triangles, (c) _____
                       PLURAL NOUN

2. Which _____ -*rats* parent has _____ orange
            NOUN   ADJECTIVE

   hair? (a) Stu, (b) Didi, (c) Charlotte

3. Daggett Beaver's middle name is . . . (a) _____ ,
                                              CELEBRITY

   (b) Doofus, (c) Dorcas

4. A common Nigel _____ -berry phrase is . . .
                    NOUN

   (a) _____ , (b) Smashing, (c) Crashing
       VERB ENDING IN "ING"

If you guessed *b* for all _____ questions, _____ !
                           NUMBER   EXCLAMATION

You really know your Nicktoons! If not, _____ some
                                          VERB

_____ and cancel your plans, because you're in need of
TYPE OF FOOD

a/an _____ 90s marathon!
      FIRST NAME